Being thankful leads to happiness, here and now.
Saying "thank you" with the alphabet shows me how.

ABC
Thankful Me

POW!

Brooklyn, NY

WRITTEN BY
KYAW LIN

ILLUSTRATED BY
YULIYA PIELETSKAYA

A is for artwork. Thank you, artwork.

I draw and paint from my big, beating heart
because I was born to make bold, daring art.

B is for birthday.
Thank you, birthday.

I'm one year older, a lot wiser too.
Here is my chance to start something new.

C is for courage.
Thank you, courage.

Although it's okay to be afraid,
I find strength within me to be very brave.

D is for dancing. Thank you, dancing.

I shake my hips and swing them side to side.
Life is a dance, so dance and feel alive.

E is for evening.
Thank you, evening.

A gorgeous sunset floods the golden sky.
I lie on sunlit grass till stars come by.

F is for friendship.
Thank you, friendship.

My besties let me be my silly self.
I can depend on them like no one else.

G is for garden.
Thank you, garden.

I have dirt on my hands, more on my knees.
When my feet kiss the Earth, I feel at ease.

H is for hardship.
Thank you, hardship.

MATH CH. 2

MATH QUIZ

If I'm knocked down,
I hold my head up, high.
Good things will happen
when I get back up and try.

I is for insight.
Thank you, insight.

All things turn out as they are meant to be.
I live and learn; now, I'm a better me.

J is for journey.
Thank you, journey.

I travel far; I have not gone astray.
I let my heart and conscience guide the way.

K is for kindness. Thank you, kindness.

An act of kindness can be small and sweet.
It brightens my life and all those I meet.

L is for laughter.
Thank you, laughter.

I take my pain and laugh each one out.
Laughing can be healing; there's no doubt.

M is for moonlight. Thank you, moonlight.

When nightfall comes, and there's no
I watch the bright moon as it wat

N is for nature. Thank you, nature.

The birds are graceful, gliding in the breeze.
I'm in pure bliss among the lakes and trees.

O is for ocean. Thank you, ocean.

The ocean's beauty stretches far and wide.
I flow with life's ups and downs like the waves and tide.

P is for playlist.
Thank you, playlist.

I have a list of songs I play each day.
Some rock, pop, and hip-hop blasting away.

Q is for question.
Thank you, question.

I push myself as far as I can go.
I'm not afraid to ask what I don't know.

R is for rainbow. Thank you, rainbow.

The arc of colors in the sky, so bright,
fills me with hope that the world is alright.

S is for silence.
Thank you, silence.

I quiet noisy thoughts so I can hear.
There is great wisdom in me, loud and clear.

T is for teamwork.
Thank you, teamwork.

Whatever our future has in store.
we'll work together to accomplish more.

U is for unknown.
Thank you, unknown.

I trust myself; I close my eyes and leap.
Big risk, big reward, so I dive in deep.

V is for veggies. Thank you, veggies.

I eat good food to take care of myself.
Kale, peas, and carrots are good for my health.

W is for weekend.
Thank you, weekend.

I am so glad to wrap up a long week.
On my days off, I tend to over-sleep.

X is for x-ray.
Thank you, x-ray.

The x-ray shows bones, my insides lay bare.
It can't show love, but I know love is there.

Y is for yoga.
Thank you, yoga.

I stretch to balance my body and mind.
The present moment leaves worries behind.

Z is for zen.
Thank you, zen.

I breathe in gratitude and breathe out love.
I'm one with the world and stars above.

ABC Thankful Me

Text © 2022 Kyaw Lin
Illustrations © 2022 Yuliya Pieletskaya

Published by POW!
a division of powerHouse Packaging & Supply, Inc.
32 Adams Street, Brooklyn, NY 11201-1021

www.POWkidsbooks.com
Distributed by powerHouse Books
www.powerHouseBooks.com

First edition, 2022

Library of Congress Control Number: 2021937358

ISBN 978-1-57687-999-3

Printed by Toppan Leefung

10 9 8 7 6 5 4 3 2 1

Printed and bound in China

Kyaw Lin immigrated to the United States from Myanmar
at the age of seven, barely speaking a word of English.
Determined to learn the new language, he spent most
of his childhood visiting public libraries in Queens, New
York. After stumbling upon numerous romantic novels
and human anatomy books, he would later come home
with various uncomfortable questions for his parents.
These days, he continues to visit local libraries. However,
his wife and two know-it-all sons
now accompany him.

Yuliya Pieletskaya is a children's book illustrator and
3D environmental artist. Originally from Odessa, Ukraine,
she immigrated to upstate New York at the age of 9.
She currently lives in Chicago with her husband and
two bunnies. In her spare time, she wanders the prairies
of Illinois, looking for birds, flowers and bunnies to
admire from afar. She is passionate about protecting
all of America's public lands and wildlife, as well
as environmental justice.
This is her second published book.

`v`/`w` Page torn out. -KCA

E LIN
Lin, Kyaw
ABC thankful me

5/23